I0057095

se

A must-read for leaders in finance. Hood and Fookes provide not only insights but also the confidence to navigate the future of our industry with data at the forefront.
Ben Mariano | Founder, Tehol & Bugg

Hood and Fookes have written the definitive guide on why finance should own data. Their practical insights are invaluable for finance professionals at any stage of their career
Shayne Kong | President, SkyBridge Digital Solutions

Hood and Fookes don't just explain why finance should own data—they show exactly how to turn it into a strategic advantage. Packed with insights, real-world case studies, and actionable strategies, this book gives finance professionals the confidence and tools to lead with data
Jeremy Harris | Co-Founder, SkySight Analytics

I couldn't put this book down. Hood and Fookes show exactly how data transforms profitability and strategy in finance. Inspiring and practical.
Carl Grant III | Author, *How to Live the Abundant Life*

Who Moved My Data? is the guide I wish I had years ago. Hood and Fookes explain the critical role data plays in finance with precision and clarity.
Aaron Poynton | Author, *Think Like A Black Sheep*

Greg Hood and Craig Fookes are pioneers, and their book is a testament to their vision. *Who Moved My Data?* is the handbook for finance professionals in the modern age.
Casel Burnett | Vice President, LODI, and International Bestselling Author of *No Regrets*

WHO MOVED MY DATA?

DATA-DRIVEN STRATEGIES IN MODERN FINANCE

CRAIG FOOKES AND
GREG HOOD

Leaders
Press

Copyright © 2025 Greg Hood and Craig Fookes
Published in the United States by Leaders Press.
www.leaderspress.com

All rights reserved. No part of this book may be reproduced or
transmitted in any form or by any means, electronic or mechanical,
including photocopying, recording, or by an information storage and
retrieval system – except by a reviewer who may quote brief passages in
a review to be printed in a magazine or newspaper – without permission
in writing from the copyright holder.

All trademarks, service marks, trade names, product names, and logos
appearing in this publication are the property of their respective owners.

ISBN (pbk) 978-1-63735-374-5
ISBN (ebook) 978-1-63735-373-8

Library of Congress Control Number: 2025903456

Dedication

To our fellow finance professionals, we dedicate this guide as a bridge between steadfast traditions and the dynamic world of data. May it inspire you to harness the power of data, enriching your thoughts and careers.

Foreword

The ability for emerging financial professionals who can unlock the insights they obtain from greater data intimacy is an inexpensive but powerful way to position your organization for increased success in the marketplace and to ensure your services are indispensable to your employer.

– Brent Zorgdrager
Chair of the Audit, Finance, and Risk
Committee at the Financial Services
Regulatory Authority of Ontario.
Former Chair of the Audit Committee
at Qtrade Securities Inc.

Table of Contents

Introduction

"Data is the new currency in finance; neglect it, and you're turning away from tomorrow's wealth."
—Greg Hood

This is not a how-to book; it's a "why" book for finance professionals. It explains why you need to embrace data and encourages you to embrace it, whether you are a recent graduate or a seasoned veteran looking to reinvent yourself. The role of finance professionals is fundamentally transforming in this era of technology. The essence of this shift is that understanding data is not optional but necessary for every finance professional. In this digital era, finance transcends the mundane arithmetic of yesteryears.

Today's finance professionals must harness the power of data, transforming it from raw numbers into strategic insights. For instance, consider how data-driven insights have revolutionized investment strategies, enabling traders to predict market trends with unprecedented accuracy. Our mission in this discourse is to illuminate the profound significance of data in finance, establishing it as an indispensable tool in the arsenal of every finance practitioner.

It is a fallacy to perceive data as solely a technological entity confined within the parameters of information technology (IT). This misconception undermines the strategic potential of data, which is inherently intertwined with financial acumen. The actual value of data is unlocked only when melded with the analytical prowess and economic insights inherent to finance professionals. This is not to say that IT has no role in managing data. On the contrary, IT provides the infrastructure and tools necessary for data management. However, when collected and interpreted by those with financial expertise, data can yield insights far beyond the scope of traditional IT.

The integration of data into finance necessitates a reevaluation of the conventional IT structure. It's essential to bifurcate the concept of IT into two distinct yet interconnected aspects: information and technology. While *technology* refers to the tools and platforms for data processing, the *information* concerns the data itself: its analysis, interpretation, and strategic financial application.

In this divergence, finance professionals must gravitate towards the *information* aspect, harnessing data for insights, forecasts, and strategic decisions. It's about elevating from mere data entry or software use to strategic data analysis and application.

Data is a significant business asset, comparable to a fixed asset on a balance sheet, underscoring its potential for future monetization and its profound impact on financial strategies and outcomes. Unlike traditional assets, data's value multiplies as it is used effectively, making its proper management and analysis a critical function within the finance department. The role of data has evolved from a mere support function to a core strategic asset, a transition that underscores its substantial value in driving business decisions and enhancing profitability.

Data systems are not just operational tools but also assets with tangible value. When developed and maintained with strategic intent, these systems can become fixed assets, providing long-term value and potential for future sales.

The potential for monetizing data assets at a future date cannot be overstated. In parallel to real estate investment, where a property's value appreciates over time, data assets, when nurtured and optimized, offer lucrative opportunities for future transactions. This appreciation hinges on the quality of data and the insights it can generate, making it a coveted asset in the finance industry.

Don't Be a Dinosaur!

The stark reality is that finance professionals who need to adapt to the data-centric world risk becoming obsolete. The digital era has ushered in a tidal wave of change, transforming data into the *slang* of the business world. For finance professionals, remaining detached from this sea of change is akin to navigating treacherous waters without a compass.

The urgency to become data-literate is not merely about staying afloat but charting a course toward new horizons of opportunity and innovation. As data becomes the cornerstone of financial decision-making, the lack of proficiency in understanding and leveraging this vital resource leads to diminishing relevance in the industry.

The specter of professional obsolescence looms large for those in the finance sector who fail to embrace data literacy. Analogous to the evolution of species, just as adaptability is critical to survival, finance professionals must adapt by integrating data literacy into their skill set. This evolution is not about replacing traditional financial acumen but rather about enriching it with the power of data analysis and interpretation.

The combination of financial expertise and data literacy creates a formidable toolset, enabling professionals to offer deeper insights, forecast trends more accurately, and contribute more significantly to strategic decision-making.

For today's finance practitioners, data literacy is as fundamental as understanding financial principles. It is the new currency in a data-rich world, where the ability to decipher, analyze, and interpret data sets leaders apart from followers. This literacy enables practitioners to extract meaningful insights from vast data sets, transforming raw numbers into strategic assets that can guide business decisions and drive growth.

Craig Fookes: A Blend of Finance and Data Expertise

"Innovation in finance is about more than numbers; it's about shaping the future with data."
—Craig Fookes

Craig Fookes has had a distinguished career in the financial sector for over thirty-five years. He obtained his certified management accountant (CMA) designation in 1992 and has worked across various pillars of the financial industry. His experience includes roles in banking, insurance, venture capital, asset management, online brokerage, advisory brokerage, and the Robo channel. Craig has successfully navigated the evolving regulatory environment of the financial services industry, finding both challenges and rewards in this dynamic field.

In the latter part of his career, Craig focused on the Canadian financial small- and medium-sized business (SMB) space. During this period, he was pivotal in completing four mergers and acquisition (M&A) transactions amid significant industry consolidation. A strong advocate for the use of data and analytics in financial processes and systems, Craig worked closely with finance and IT teams to develop comprehensive data flows from the core to economic systems. This effort led to his team being named the "Most Innovative Finance Team 2016" by *Wealth & Finance International*.

It's important to note that Craig initially came up through the accounting and internal control system side of finance. He began involving himself with finance's technology and data aspects later in his career, recognizing the niche and advantages in this area. Despite starting later in the data realm compared to his colleague Greg, Craig has made significant contributions and advancements in integrating data and technology in financial processes.

Greg Hood: Pioneering Data in Finance

"In the tapestry of finance, each data thread weaves a story of opportunity and growth."
—Greg Hood

A prominent figure in Toronto, Canada's finance and data sector, Hood has made significant strides in integrating technology and finance. He is distinguished as one of the first certified public accountants (CPAs) to hold the title of chief data officer (CDO) in Canada, blending his CPA background with data expertise.

His pioneering work includes the development of an SQL-based data warehouse, a project that unified various databases and Excel spreadsheets into a single, efficient system. This endeavor set a new standard in North American costing databases and significantly boosted the company's business intelligence (BI) capabilities.

Hood's foresight is further exemplified in the successful implementation of a NetSuite enterprise resource planning (ERP) system, achieved in a remarkable seventy-five days, and the creation of a comprehensive data warehouse and data lake. These initiatives have greatly enhanced organizational reporting capabilities and transformed raw data into valuable business insights.

Recognized for his innovative efforts, Hood and his team were awarded the "Most Innovative Finance Department" in 2016 by *Wealth & Finance International*. His work has also earned performance awards at prestigious organizations such as NEI, AGF Investments, Canada Life, and Qtrade.

Moreover, Hood extends his expertise beyond professional realms, mentoring CPA students and contributing to nurturing future finance professionals. His journey underscores his role as a visionary at the nexus of finance and data, driving the industry forward through his commitment to innovative technology and data analytics.

The Convergence of Financial Designations and Data Proficiency

In our previous data, finance, and reporting team, over 75 percent brought more than technical acumen to the table; they hold prestigious financial designations like certified public accountant (CPA), chartered financial analyst (CFA), and master of business administration (MBA). This blend of data expertise and financial knowledge is necessary for navigating today's complex economic landscape.

A CPA's proficiency in financial and management reporting, tax laws, and auditing offers a solid foundation for nuanced financial data analysis. CFAs, with their deep understanding of investment analysis and portfolio management, provide critical insights into investment opportunities and market risks. MBAs, equipped with a broad spectrum of business knowledge, strategic thinking, and operational insights, use data to propel strategic decisions and enhance business processes.

This fusion of financial designations with data roles transcends traditional data processing and evolves into strategic data intelligence. This represents a fundamental shift necessary in the data-driven financial world we navigate today, emphasizing the critical role of these qualifications in economic decision-making and strategy formulation.

In financial data analysis, coding involves the technical creation of algorithms and contextualizing data within the economic narrative. Armed with vital financial designations, our team excels in this critical dimension. They elevate coding from mere programming to insightful analysis, interpreting and contextualizing data to transform it into actionable financial intelligence. This approach ensures that coding in finance goes beyond syntax and structure, delving into the strategic implications of data. We also ensure that we avoid the pitfall of coding without context.

Craig's Mergers & Acquisitions (M&A) Mastery Through Data

From my early days as a CMA, I quickly realized that traditional finance roles were evolving. The turning point in my career came when I began integrating data analytics into financial processes. I recall a pivotal project early in my tenure at a financial SMB, where we faced a complex merger. The intricate web of financial data seemed daunting, but it was a goldmine waiting to be explored. Facing a maze of financial complexities, I leveraged my deep understanding of data analytics to navigate the intricacies of the deal.

By employing targeted data analysis, I was able to identify undervalued assets, uncover hidden liabilities, and negotiate a more favorable deal structure. This data-driven approach expedited the M&A process and added substantial value to the transaction, illustrating the profound impact of data literacy in high-stakes financial negotiations.

Greg's Innovative Data Warehouse Implementation

My journey in finance has been a blend of traditional accounting and the avant-garde world of data. As one of the first CPAs in Canada to become a CDO, I've witnessed firsthand the transformative power of data in finance. A landmark project in my career was the creation of an SQL-based data warehouse for a leading financial institution.

This project consolidated disparate data sources, transforming a fragmented data landscape into a cohesive, efficient system. The impact was immediate: streamlined reporting processes, enhanced decision-making, and a culture shift towards data-driven insights. This endeavor was more than just an IT project; it was a strategic move that redefined how the institution approached data. It merged data, accounting, and financial planning & analysis (FP&A), all interconnected with data flowing across systems. This was feasible as it was finance-driven and not IT-driven.

Another standout moment was implementing a comprehensive data warehouse at a leading financial institution. Faced with disjointed and inefficient data systems, I spearheaded the development of a unified data warehouse that integrated disparate data sources into a cohesive framework. This innovation significantly streamlined reporting processes, enhanced decision-making accuracy, and fostered a culture of data-driven insights within the organization. The project improved operational efficiency and transformed the institution's approach to data management, setting a new industry standard.

Our Collective Insights

Together, our experiences underscore a universal truth: data literacy is no longer a luxury in finance; it's a necessity. Whether it's navigating mergers, designing data warehouses, or transforming internal processes, the ability to understand and leverage data has been a cornerstone of our success.

Our journey is a testament to the evolving landscape of finance, where data literacy is as critical as traditional financial acumen. As we share these stories, we aim to inspire finance professionals to embrace the world of data analytics, not just as a skill but as an essential part of their professional identity. In the ever-changing world of finance, those who can harness the power of data will lead the charge into the future.

The Case Studies

The transformative impact of data-driven approaches in the finance sector is evident across various scenarios, illustrating a paradigm shift in operational efficiency and strategic decision-making.

Investment Advisor Commission Payments: A Testament to Data-Driven Efficiency

In the case of investment advisor commission payments, the integration of data analytics revolutionized the entire process, serving as an example of how understanding data yields tangible results.

Situation Before Data Implementation:

- The traditional method involved manual entry, verification, and reconciliation processes.
- The average time to close monthly books was fifteen days.

Introducing Data Analytics:

- We implemented a data-driven approach, integrating automated data collection, analysis, and reporting systems.
- This transformation hinged on real-time data capture, streamlined data flows, and automated reconciliation processes.

Results Post-Data Implementation:

- The time required to close monthly books was dramatically reduced to just seven days, marking a decrease of over 50%.
- Error rates in commission calculations dropped significantly due to automated checks and balances.

Quantifiable Gains:

- Reduction in book-closing time: From fifteen days to seven days.
- Decrease manual reconciliation hours by 60%.
- Increase in overall financial reporting accuracy by 95%.
- The reconciliation process went from 2.5 days to 2.5 hours.

The benefits of this approach extended beyond just saving time. By closing books faster, the finance team could provide timely financial insights, aiding swift strategic decision-making. Furthermore, reducing manual labor and error rates translated into cost savings and enhanced employee satisfaction, as the team could focus on more strategic tasks rather than mundane data entry.

Transforming Profitability Analysis With Data: Qtrade Example

In our experiences within the financial sector, we have consistently seen how a deep understanding of data can revolutionize profitability analysis. Let's consider the example of Qtrade, where we implemented a cost-per-trade analysis.

Before Data-Driven Analysis:

- Profitability evaluation was based on general estimates and lacked the granularity necessary for strategic decision-making.
- The absence of detailed data insights led to a broad-brush approach to cost management and investment decisions.

Implementing Data-Driven Profitability Analysis:

- We introduced a comprehensive data analysis framework that examined every aspect of trading operations.
- The cost-per-trade analysis was meticulously developed, capturing each trade's direct and indirect costs.

Results and Insights:

- The data-driven approach highlighted specific areas where costs could be reduced without impacting service quality.
- We identified underperforming products and services, either improved or phased out, enhancing overall profitability.

Quantifiable Impact:

- Reduction in operational costs by 20% per trade, leading to an overall increase in profit margins.
- Identifying and eliminating 15% of underperforming trade services, leading to better resource allocation.

Line of Business (LOB) Profitability Enhancement

Our approach to LOB profitability further exemplifies the power of data. By dissecting each line of business through a data lens, we could identify profitability drivers and underperforming segments.

Data-Driven Strategy for LOB:

- We developed a model that accurately attributed revenue and costs to each LOB.
- The model provided insights into customer behavior, product performance, and operational efficiency.

Enhancing Profitability:

- The insights allowed us to realign resources towards high-performing LOBs and restructure or discontinue less profitable ones.
- We could tailor products and services to meet customer needs more effectively, increasing customer satisfaction and loyalty.

Strategic Outcomes:

- Improvement in overall LOB profitability by 30% within a year.
- Enhanced decision-making regarding investment, resource allocation, and strategic planning based on concrete data insights.

These case studies collectively highlight the crucial role of data proficiency in enhancing efficiency, profitability, and strategic decision-making in finance. They underscore the fundamental necessity of data literacy in the modern financial sector, affirming that the future of successful financial management is indelibly linked to the ability to leverage data-driven insights.

Chapter 2

What Is Data: Intro to Data, No Excel

....

"In modern finance, data is the compass that guides decision-making, not an ancillary tool."
—Craig Fookes & Greg Hood

....

The Backbone of Data Management

While this is not a technical book, as a finance professional, you should understand some of the standard tools. A *data warehouse* is an extensive electronic repository where an organization stores its accumulated data. Think of it like a vast digital library, archiving data from different sources into a single comprehensive system. Its role is akin to a central nervous system in data management, providing a structured environment for storing, retrieving, and managing large datasets.

A *data lake* is a vast pool of raw, unstructured data stored in its natural format. Picture it as a reservoir, collecting data in its most authentic form without predefined schemas. Its advantage lies in its flexibility and capacity to store massive volumes of diverse data, offering a rich resource for advanced analytics and machine learning. Navigating a data lake can be daunting due to its sheer size and unstructured nature, presenting data quality and retrieval challenges.

Data modeling is creating a data model to store the data in a database. This is akin to drafting a detailed architectural blueprint before constructing a building. A well-designed schema is crucial, serving as a framework that organizes and defines the relationships between data types.

Business intelligence (BI) reporting involves tools and processes that transform raw data into meaningful, actionable insights. It's the art of converting raw data into a compelling narrative. BI tools are like lenses that bring clarity to the otherwise blurry mass of data, enabling data-driven decision-making.

Master data management (MDM) refers to the practices, tools, and processes that ensure the uniformity, accuracy, stewardship, and consistency of an enterprise's official shared master data assets. MDM is like a conductor in an orchestra, providing all sections (data sources) play in harmony and synchronization.

In its raw form, data is "dumb" and requires business logic to make it worthwhile. It's like having a gold mine, but I need to know how to extract the gold. Assigning data ownership and applying business logic is essential to extract value from this data.

Level 1 Basic	Level 2 Opportunistic	Level 3 Systematic	Level 4 Differentiating	Level 5 Transformational
• Data is not exploited, it is used • D&A is managed in silos • People argue about whose data is correct	• IT attempts to formalize information availability requirements • Progress is hampered by culture; inconsistent incentives	• Different content types are still treated differently • Strategy and vision formed (five pages)	• Executives champion and communicate best practices	• D&A is central to business strategy
	• Organizational barriers and lack of leadership	• Agile emerges • Exogenous data sources are readily integrated	• Business-led/ driven, with CDO • D&A is an indispensable fuel for performance and innovation, and linked across programs	• Data value influences investments • Strategy and execution aligned and continually improved
• Analysis is ad hoc • Spreadsheet and information firefighting • Transactional	• Strategy is over 100 pages; not business-relevant • Data quality and insight efforts, but still in silos	• Business executives become D&A champions	• Program mgmt.. mentality for ongoing synergy • Link to outcome and data used for ROI	• Outside-in perspective • CDO sits on board

© 2017 Gartner, Inc.

Excel in Finance: A Tool, Not a Solution

Excel's popularity in finance is attributed to its familiarity and flexibility. However, it has its challenges. Excel is akin to a Swiss Army knife: versatile but only sometimes the best tool for every job.

Excel's limitations become apparent in scalability and automation. It's like using a rowboat to cross an ocean; it works for short distances but isn't feasible for more extensive journeys.

The staggering statistic that 88% of all Excel spreadsheets contain errors underscores the need for more robust, reliable tools in finance. Excel is a tool, not our only tool, and should never be a process in itself.

As finance professionals, we stand at the threshold of a data-driven era. It's time to broaden our horizons beyond traditional tools like Excel and venture into the vast possibilities that data analytics and BI reporting offer. The journey from being mere data users to becoming architects of data-driven strategies is exciting and essential for the finance professionals of tomorrow.

Chapter 3

Finance and Data Overlap: Why Finance Owns Data

"We were no longer mere recorders of financial history; we had become its interpreters and, in some ways, its predictors."
—Craig Fookes

ANALYTICAL

80%
BUSINESS
ACUMEN

ROLE PROGRESSION

ROLE PROGRESSION

80% DATA ENTRY

SUBSTANTIVE

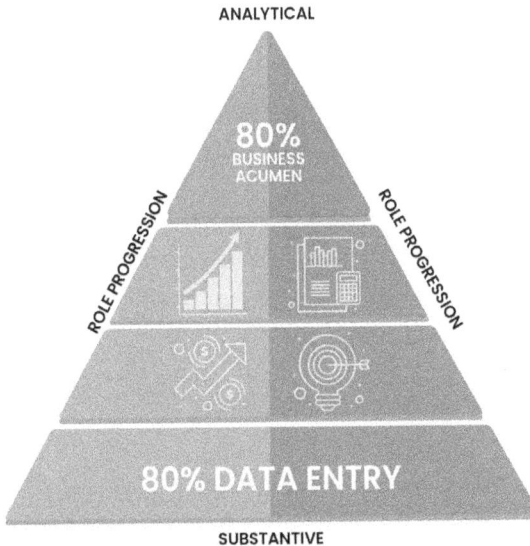

The Evolving Role of Finance Professionals

There was a time when the quintessence of a finance professional lay in their accounting prowess. Meticulous ledger entries, scrupulous balance sheets, and the ability to navigate through the labyrinth of accounting rules were the prized skills. This era was where accountants and finance professionals were the revered custodians of fiscal accuracy and regulatory compliance, a role that defined the very essence of the industry.

However, as the digital age dawned, the landscape shifted dramatically. The advent of sophisticated accounting software transformed the traditional role of accountants. These technological advancements automated many manual tasks that once defined accounting expertise. This shift raised pivotal questions about the evolving role of finance professionals in an era where algorithms and software could handle complex calculations and data management with unprecedented precision.

Accountants must evolve with time and find additional ways to add value; data is one way. This automation wave ushered in a necessity for finance professionals to adapt and evolve. Relying solely on traditional accounting skills was no longer sufficient in this rapidly changing business environment. Here, data emerged as a new frontier for value addition. For instance, understanding customer behavior patterns from sales data can help devise more effective marketing strategies. Interpreting market trends from financial data can guide investment decisions. Leveraging operational data can optimize business processes.

Data has become a skill as crucial as the age-old art of balancing books. Finance professionals are no longer just accountants and auditors; we have become data scientists, strategists, and storytellers. Our role now extends beyond balancing books and ensuring fiscal accuracy. We are equipped to extract powerful insights from the vast amounts of data available, use these insights to drive strategic decisions, and tell compelling stories about our organization's financial health and prospects.

The Vital Role of Finance Data in Decision-Making

At its core, financial data plays a pivotal role in organizational decision-making. It's not just about collecting and analyzing data; it's about transforming it into actionable insights that drive business strategy and outcomes. Therefore, finance professionals must be adept at data analysis and translating these analyses into strategic decisions that align with the organization's objectives.

The future is already unfolding, with emerging technologies like artificial intelligence (AI) and machine learning rapidly reshaping finance. Data and technology will be at the core of financial strategy, demanding that professionals constantly evolve their skills. The future chief financial officer (CFO) will need equal prowess in financial and data acumen.

The most crucial aspect of a finance professional's role in the age of data is synthesizing financial data into coherent, actionable insights. This involves understanding the numbers and the story they tell about the organization's health, opportunities, and challenges.

This integration of finance and data is reshaping the landscape of business strategy, further underscoring the vital role of finance professionals in the age of data-driven decision-making.

In finance, the conversation around data shifted from sheer volume to the "right size" data concept. This paradigm shift meant prioritizing relevant, timely, and actionable data over the accumulation of vast, often unstructured, data sets. In finance, it's not about having an ocean of data but rather having the correct data drops to quench the thirst for meaningful financial insights and decisions.

The key is honing in on relevant, high-quality data: *rightsizing* rather than accumulating vast information. Targeted data analytics allows professionals to glean sharper, more focused, actionable insights.

The true essence of finance data lies in its ability to guide business strategy and decision-making. By analyzing trends across sectors, professionals can identify new market opportunities, optimize operations, and mitigate risks. The power of finance data is in interpreting it to craft insightful, pragmatic strategies.

At the heart of finance lies a specific kind of data: finance data. These are not just numbers on a spreadsheet; they represent the bloodline of business strategy and growth. This data informs critical decisions, shapes organizational direction, and is central to financial analysis and decision-making.

Being data literate is now as crucial as being financially savvy. Discerning patterns and narratives hidden within data allows finance professionals to anticipate market movements and confidently make strategic decisions. Data literacy becomes a game-changer by understanding what happened in the past and what might happen in the future.

In light of the above, it becomes evident why data ownership should naturally reside within the finance domain. Data is about output, and that output is numbers, financial analysis, and business.

Ultimately, the raison d'être of data in the finance sector is to facilitate meaningful outcomes. This includes numbers that lead to insightful financial analysis and informed business decisions. This reality underscores the argument for the natural residency of data within the finance domain. With their profound understanding of business economics and financial principles, finance professionals are uniquely positioned to interpret and apply data in ways that drive organizational value. Their expertise goes beyond mere number crunching; it encompasses a deep understanding of how data relates to financial health and corporate strategy.

The intersection of finance and data is more than just a passing trend; it's a fundamental shift in how finance operates in the modern business landscape. The future of finance lies in its ability to integrate data into every aspect of its functioning, from decision-making to strategy formulation.

To aspiring professionals, the baton is in your hands. Embrace this data-driven future with excitement and determination. Acquire the knowledge and skills to harness data, drive decisions, and lead the finance industry into this new era. The future of finance will be defined by those who can extract strategic insights from data. Are you ready to take up the challenge?

Data Monetization: A New Era in Finance

Exploring the potential for data monetization opens a new frontier for finance professionals. The ability to convert data into revenue streams or cost-saving opportunities represents a paradigm shift.

As we continue to explore the interplay between finance and data, it becomes increasingly clear that the future of finance is inextricably linked to its ability to adapt to and embrace the world of data analytics.

Data monetization represents a significant paradigm shift in the finance sector. This isn't just about turning numbers into insights; it's about turning insights into tangible, measurable value. With their inherent understanding of business metrics and economic trends, finance professionals are well-positioned to harness data's power for revenue generation and cost optimization.

Strategies for Value Generation From Data

By organizing your data, hashing, and anonymizing it, you can put your data sets onto third-party data marketplaces. Think of it like a stock market or Amazon of data sets. Finance teams have a wealth of rich data they can put up for sale (of course, following all data and privacy regulations) and turn finance into a profit center instead of a cost center. Typical customers are hedge fund managers and academia/researchers.

Predictive analytics for revenues: By analyzing historical data, finance professionals can better predict future sales and revenues and make informed decisions. This proactive approach can lead to more accurate budgeting and forecasting; the business will know where to spend its money.

Risk management: Utilizing data for risk assessment allows for a more nuanced understanding of potential pitfalls, enabling better risk management strategies and safeguarding against significant financial losses.

One thing all future CFOs will face is M&A work. Without having readily available access to data that is accurate and can be sliced and diced in numerous views, the M&A process is fraught with risks and hardships. Not only does it take longer to close a deal (and time equals deal risk), but in a recent survey by SkySight Analytics, the cost of having poor, inaccurate data quality can be as much as $5 million on a mid-market deal (representing about 10 percent of the transaction price). $5 million... That is a very significant number and represents the holy grail of data monetization.

Chapter 4

Futures

....

*"In the evolving tableau of finance, those who harness data hold the key
to the future."*
—Craig Fookes & Greg Hood

....

A Significant Transformation

The roles of CFOs and CDOs are undergoing a significant transformation. This change emphasizes the need for data literacy and the integration of data-driven methodologies in strategic decision-making.

The traditional role of the CFO as a fiscal guardian is evolving into a dynamic position that requires navigating the complexities of data-driven finance. This transformation is comparable to the shift from analog to digital, with CFOs needing to embed data analytics into their strategic framework. The modern CFO's role transcends traditional fiscal stewardship, demanding a deep understanding of data analytics to inform strategic decisions and drive business growth.

Although relatively recent, the CDO role has become pivotal in finance. CDOs are tasked with the governance and innovation of data strategies, shaping critical business decisions. They are explorers in the data realm, steering the course of data governance and harnessing its potential to inform and influence strategic business outcomes.

In SMBs, merging the CFO and CDO roles offers significant advantages, combining financial acumen with data expertise. This dual role demands balancing two critical aspects: financial management and data-driven innovation. The emergence of finance professionals as CDOs highlights the growing importance of data literacy, positioning it as a crucial skill for future finance leaders.

Transitioning "Old School" CFOs to the New Era

The transition of traditional CFOs to this new data-centric era is vital. Their reluctance to embrace data-driven changes is akin to navigating modern finance with outdated tools. The integration of automated financial analysis transforms the CFO role from traditional number crunching to strategic business partnerships, emphasizing the need for a forward-thinking approach in financial management.

The future of finance is increasingly intertwined with data literacy and AI integration. The roles of CFOs and CDOs are expanding to include strategic data management, positioning them as key players in shaping the future of finance. As the industry evolves, finance professionals must embrace this change, ensuring their skills and roles align with the demands of a data-driven financial landscape. The success of finance professionals in this new era will depend on their ability to adapt and thrive in a world where data is a central pillar of strategic decision-making.

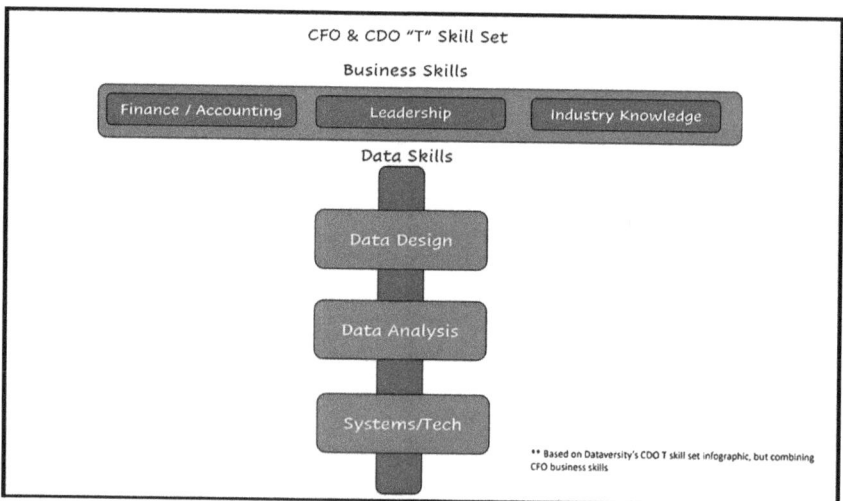

CFO & CDO "T" Skill Set

Business Skills

| Finance / Accounting | Leadership | Industry Knowledge |

Data Skills

Data Design

Data Analysis

Systems/Tech

** Based on Dataversity's CDO T skill set infographic, but combining CFO business skills

Integration of AI and Automated Financial Analysis

AI is set to revolutionize the finance sector. AI's ability to analyze large datasets, identify patterns, and make predictions transforms financial analysis, risk management, and decision-making processes.

Automated financial analysis, powered by AI, enables finance professionals to process and analyze data quickly and accurately. This automation frees up time for CFOs and finance teams to focus on more strategic tasks, such as interpreting the data and making informed business decisions.

AI-driven tools also enhance predictive analytics, enabling finance professionals to forecast future trends accurately. This predictive capability is invaluable in risk assessment and strategic planning, allowing companies to be more proactive and less reactive in their financial decisions.

As we look to the future, it's evident that a data-centric approach will define the finance sector. CFOs and CDOs will increasingly collaborate to drive data strategy, leveraging AI and automated analysis to gain deeper insights and drive business growth.

Finance professionals must adapt to this new landscape by developing data literacy and embracing technology. The ability to interpret and leverage data and integrate AI into financial processes will be critical skills.

The future of finance is exciting and filled with opportunities for those who embrace the power of data. The roles of CFOs and CDOs are becoming more intertwined, and AI is set to play a pivotal role in reshaping the industry. As Hood mentions, "Whoever owns data will also own AI in the future."

Chapter 5

Finance

Use Cases

"Data is the compass that guides the ship of finance through the sea of uncertainty."
—Craig Fookes & Greg Hood

Internal Controls: Safeguarding Financial Integrity

In today's digital finance landscape, data acts as both a lighthouse and a shield, crucial in enhancing financial integrity and system controls. Data-driven internal controls are the backbone of financial integrity, guiding and safeguarding the financial processes like a lighthouse, ensuring safe navigation. Implementing data analytics allows organizations to automatically detect and flag unusual transaction patterns, thus reducing the risk of financial fraud or errors. This proactive approach is akin to a vigilant sentinel, continuously monitoring for anomalies and ensuring compliance.

Establishing a "single source of truth" in financial data management is akin to having a reliable compass for navigation. This unified approach eliminates discrepancies and inconsistencies in financial reporting, ensuring all stakeholders make decisions based on consistent, accurate, and up-to-date information.

The focus on traditional auditing skills by audit firms often overlooks the broader scope of financial strategy and business understanding. In the era of big data, the reliance on substantive testing and manual processes is becoming archaic, much like using an outdated map. Modern data-driven audits leverage analytics to pinpoint areas of higher risk and strategic importance, enhancing the audit's efficiency and effectiveness. Audit firms are being forced to keep up with the industry clients they serve. The audit is ripe for innovation.

Data literacy is becoming increasingly crucial in the finance sector. Finance professionals must evolve to be adept at financial management and data analytics. This dual proficiency involves extracting, interpreting, and leveraging data for strategic decision-making, transforming professionals into strategists capable of guiding organizations through the data-rich landscapes of modern finance.

In summary, integrating data in finance transforms traditional practices, empowering professionals with enhanced accuracy, security, and strategic foresight. As finance continues to evolve, those proficient in data utilization will lead the way in innovation, efficiency, and compliance, cementing the role of data as a cornerstone of financial activities. We hope that by providing these stories and use cases, you, as finance professionals, will go forth and embrace data.

Welcome to a World Where Data Is Not Just a Facet of Finance But Its Cornerstone!

Acknowledgments

First, I'd like to thank my co-author and mentor, Craig. Without him taking a chance on an up-and-coming finance data professional, we wouldn't have these stories to write about. Of course, my loving wife, Anna, who encouraged me during all those rough times of fighting IT not to give up on my vision of having data and finance as one. And lastly, to my dad, who bought me a Commodore 64 back in 1981 and taught me how to code. He unwittingly set me on this path so many years ago; he was my best mentor.

About the Authors

Following a college curriculum, Craig Fookes attained his CMA designation in 1992 and has subsequently served in a variety of progressively senior finance roles.

Throughout his thirty-five-year professional tenure, Craig has enjoyed the opportunity to work in all the financial pillars. It has been both a privilege and a challenge to experience banking, insurance, venture capital, asset management, online brokerage, advisory brokerage, and, most recently, the Robo channel. The experiences that Craig has enjoyed have been extremely satisfying particularly with the regulatory environment that has been constantly changing and evolving.

Craig has focused the later part of his career in the Canadian Financial SMB space, which has experienced significant consolidation and required him to be integral in the completion of four M&A transactions.

As a progressive financial professional, Craig has been a strong proponent of the use of data and analytics in support of financial processes, systems, and the overall control environment. Working with the finance and IT staff allowed for the development of end-to-end data flow from the core to financial systems. It culminated with his team being awarded Most Innovative Finance Team 2016 from Wealth & Finance International.

Although Craig has had a satisfying career and accolades for his work, he says his greatest reward is the long-term professional relationships developed and maintained with individuals of all backgrounds.

Greg Hood is a trailblazing figure in the realm of finance and data-driven innovation and is one of the inaugural CPAs in Canada to bear the title of CDO proudly. Gregory stands at the forefront of the data-driven finance revolution. With nearly twenty-five years of diverse experience spanning finance, business intelligence (BI), data engineering, and strategy across numerous industries, Greg is a dynamic and multi-award-winning executive whose contributions have left an indelible mark on the industry.

Greg's leadership prowess is underscored by almost two decades of management experience, during which he has demonstrated an exceptional ability to unite finance, BI, and overall organizational strategy. Greg's strategic mindset and hands-on data approach have yielded tangible results, driving work process improvements that not only enhance efficiency but also yield significant cost savings.

A specialist in BI and data engineering, Greg is celebrated for his expertise in reporting and analysis, strategy development, automation, management information systems (MIS), and financial optimization. Greg is a visionary leader who continues to shape the landscape of data-driven finance, leaving an indelible legacy of innovation and excellence.

FINANCE DATA DRIVEN INSIGHTS

FOLLOW GREG HOOD ON LINKEDIN FOR THE LATEST NEWS, UPDATES, AND INSIGHTS ON BECOMING A DATA-DRIVEN FINANCE PROFESSIONAL

SCAN TO CONNECT WITH GREG ON LINKEDIN

www.ingramcontent.com/pod-product-compliance
Lightning Source LLC
Chambersburg PA
CBHW040759220326
41597CB00029BB/5045